Bernadette Cuxart

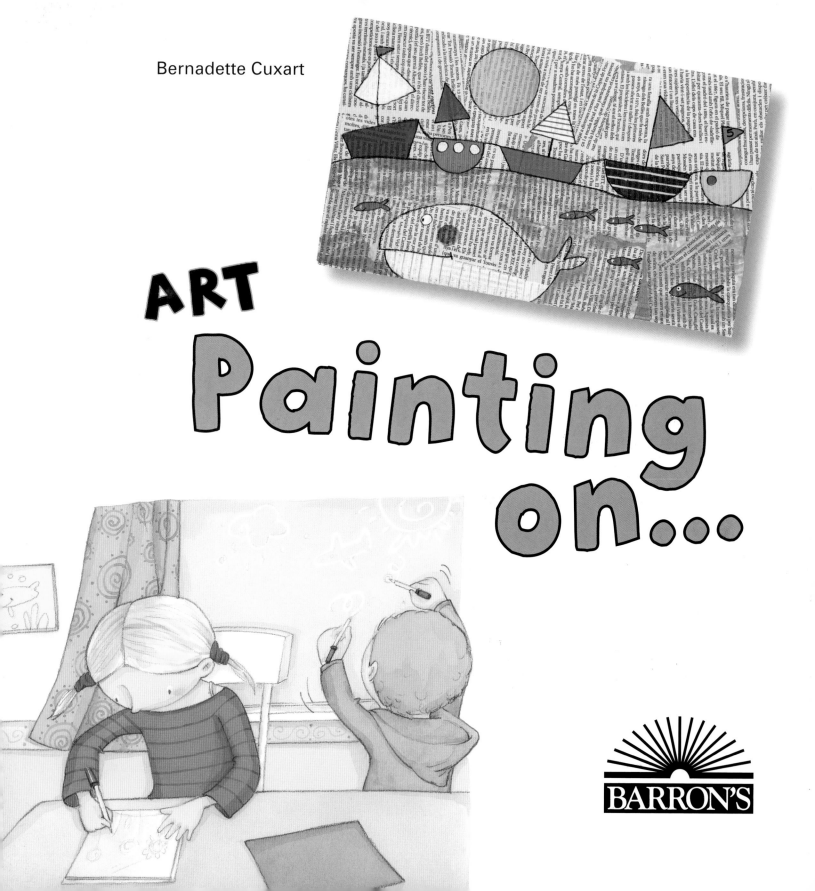

ART

Painting on...

BARRON'S

e N T S

A LITTLE HOUSE

on aluminum foil

We bet you've used aluminum foil before to make a river or a mirror. Our project today is painting on it: it can make a great sky.

MATERIALS: *Aluminum foil, cardboard, tape, a tray to mix colors, paintbrushes, paint, pencil, and paper.*

1 Make a few drawings on a sheet of paper. Then practice the one you like the best because you'll have to draw it right onto the foil.

2 Cut out a piece of aluminum a little bigger than the cardboard. Stretch it over the cardboard so that it's smooth on the front, folding over the extra edges on the back. Secure them with a few pieces of tape.

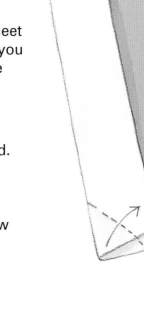

3 Get your paints ready, mixing the colors you want to use in the tray.

4 Now you're ready to paint your picture. You've been practicing and know how to do it perfectly so, go ahead!

Painting on aluminum foil is very easy. The paintbrush and paint slide so smoothly over the foil!

MATERIALS: Paper doilies or thin paper, card, scissors, roller, plastic paint tray, and a compass.

A BACKGROUND
on paper doilies

1 If you have paper doilies, jump to step 3. If you don't have any, don't worry, because they're fun and easy to make: draw a circle on some thin paper with the help of a compass. Cut it out and fold it in half, and then in half again, and so on, four times.

2 Make some random cuts and holes on each side of the triangle with the scissors as shown in the drawing. Unfold it and you have your paper doily!

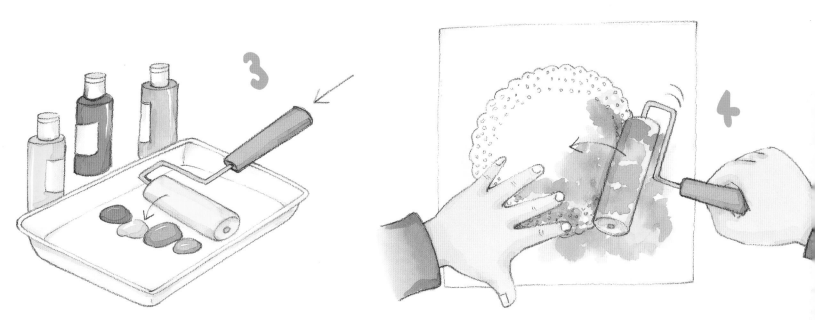

3 Pour some globs of paint in a row inside the paint tray. Move the roller over them so that it soaks up the paint.

4 Place the paper doily on the card and move the roller over it in all directions. Hold onto it with your other hand so it doesn't move. When it's all painted, remove the paper.

Isn't the background you made with the doily pretty?

on sandpaper LEAVES

You can find sandpaper in different colors and with very fine to extra coarse textures. Pick the one you like the best.

MATERIALS: Coarse-grit sandpaper, paper, crayons, and a pencil.

1

1 You should think carefully about the drawing you want to make when you are going to draw directly onto a material that cannot be erased, which is the case here. Make some sketches on another piece of paper, study the drawing and practice as long as you need to.

2

2 After you've picked your drawing, draw it directly onto the sandpaper with the crayons. Start with the outline.

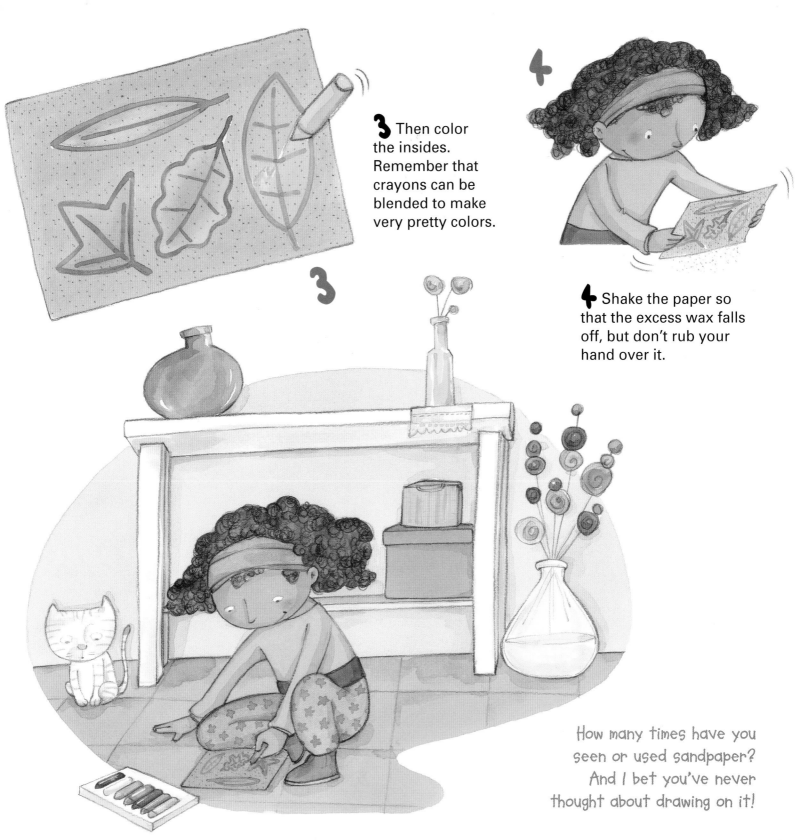

3 Then color the insides. Remember that crayons can be blended to make very pretty colors.

4 Shake the paper so that the excess wax falls off, but don't rub your hand over it.

How many times have you seen or used sandpaper? And I bet you've never thought about drawing on it!

9

A GAME on stones

Look for round flat stones: they work the best and they'll be so pretty… or even beautiful!

MATERIALS:
Stones, acrylic paint, paintbrushes, a plate or palette for mixing colors, a permanent black marker pen. Optional: varnish.

2 Prepare the paints. Use a palette to mix the colors. Paint a background color on some stones and let them dry.

1 Wash the stones and let them dry. Look at them and think about what each stone could be, what it reminds you of.

3 If one has a unique shape, use the shape to make a special drawing.

3

4 Paint motifs over the ones with backgrounds. You can use a permanent marker for the small details. If your drawings are all related, you can even use the stones to play with!

4

If you decided to use your stones as game pieces, varnish them so they last longer.

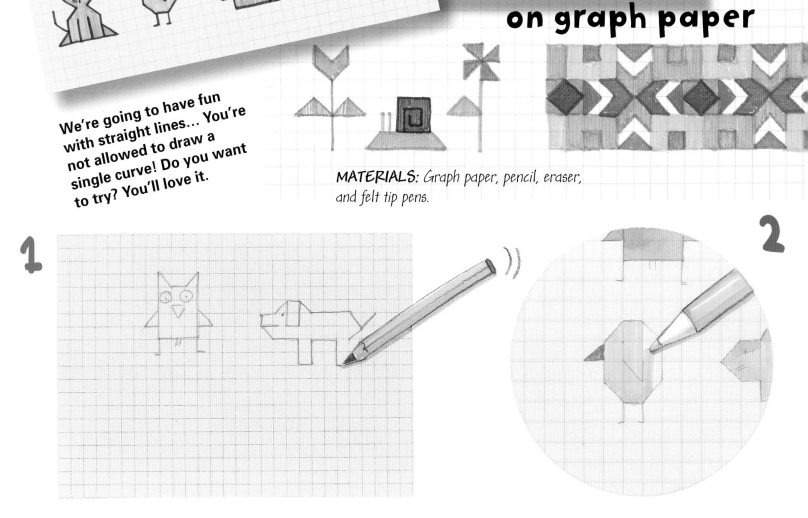

ANIMALS
on graph paper

We're going to have fun with straight lines… You're not allowed to draw a single curve! Do you want to try? You'll love it.

MATERIALS: *Graph paper, pencil, eraser, and felt tip pens.*

1 Make a few test drawings with the pencil on the graph paper. The idea is to make "pixilated" drawings, that is, using little squares or half squares to make them. Try with little animals.

2 When you've drawn several, color them in with pens. Color them going up and down to make parallel lines so that the color is uniform.

3 After you have colored them in, go over the outlines with a black pen so that they look better. If you can see pencil marks, erase them.

4 This technique also works great for making patterned borders. Think of a motif and repeat it, combining different colors.

Counting squares will be really useful for making borders and symmetric patterns.

It won't be hard for you to find leaves while you're walking to school or in a park. Try and find quite thick ones.

FISH
on leaves

MATERIALS: *Plant leaves, sheets of paper, a couple of thick books for flattening the leaves, paints, paintbrush, a dish for mixing, a sheet of cardboard, and adhesive putty.*

1 How many different shapes do the leaves you've collected have? What do they remind you of? If necessary, wash them carefully.

2 Place them neatly between two sheets of paper. Put some weight on top and leave them like that for a few days so the leaves are well pressed.

3 When they are flat, it's time to decorate them. Prepare the paints and paint the details you like to make them into whatever you want them to be. For example, the leaves could be fish because of their shape, but also many other things!

3

4

4 To finish, make a composition by sticking the leaves onto a cardboard background. You can use little balls of adhesive putty.

This mural looks like a seabed. Maybe you can find a round leaf to make a sponge or one that looks like a seashell...

15

So many letters all together in the newspaper need you to brighten them up with a drawing, one that you can do well. Shall we begin?

A LANDSCAPE
on newspaper

MATERIAL: Newspapers, cardboard, glue stick, paints, paintbrush, a graphite pencil, and a black pencil.

1 Tear off pieces of newspaper with your fingers and glue them onto the cardboard, until it's almost completely covered.

2 Make a nice drawing on it.

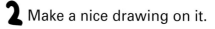

3 It's time to give it some color. You can create different effects: in some parts use very thick paint to cover the letters of the newspaper; in others, dilute the paint with a little water because it also looks nice if you can see the text. You can even leave some areas unpainted.

4 When the paper and the paint are dry, go over the outlines with a black pencil to make the drawing stand out.

Maybe before now you only used old newspapers to protect the table. Well, now you know another way to reuse them!

A FOREST of reliefs

Sometimes drawing tools are right in front of our eyes... but we don't see them.

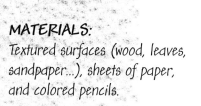

MATERIALS:
Textured surfaces (wood, leaves, sandpaper...), sheets of paper, and colored pencils.

1 Find some materials around you that have a little relief. We suggest that you try using wood, some plant leaves, and sandpaper. But also try out other things you find, like coins, walls, a straw hat... It's all about experimenting!

2 We're going to make a forest. To make the tree trunks, put a sheet of paper on the wood and rub the side of the pencil over the paper from top to bottom.

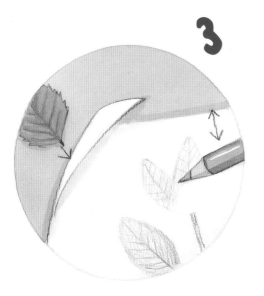

3

3 Then put the leaves under the sheet of paper where the treetops will be and rub the pencil over them in the same way. As you do this, you will see how the veins stand out on the paper.

4

4 And to finish your forest, make the ground by using the texture of sandpaper. You know how to do it now: put it under the paper and rub the side of the pencil over it.

If you look closely, you will find lots of things around you that you can use to make textures on paper with this technique. Take some paper and a pencil and try it out. It will be fun!

MAGNETS
on bottle caps

Tell the whole family! Nobody throws bottle caps away until further orders.

MATERIALS:
Soda bottle caps, nail polish, googly eyes, glue, toothpicks, and magnets.

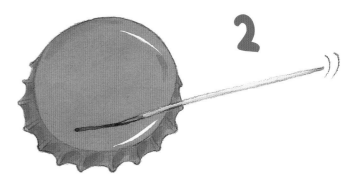

1 Paint each cap a different color. Let them dry.

2 Then, using a toothpick, draw on the faces: the mouth, the nose, and the eyes, if you like.

3 Instead of painting the eyes, you can use googly eyes. Some are self-adhesive, but if they're not, you can stick them on with a little nail polish. They're really funny!

4 And if you want to make your little faces into fridge magnets, glue a magnet onto the back.

Apart from being very cool magnets, you can use the decorated bottle caps as pieces for board games, for example.

Crumpling up paper is a really easy way of creating an original texture.

A DOVE
on crumpled paper

MATERIALS: A sheet of construction paper (Kraft, for example), a graphite pencil, a black pencil, paints, paintbrushes, and a dish.

1 Crumple up the paper into a ball.

2 Smooth it out, flattening it with your hands.

3 First make a pencil drawing and then, when you're happy with it, go over the outline in black.

4 Pour the paint colors you need into the dish and paint the inside of your drawing. If you go outside the lines a little, it doesn't matter, because you can redo the outline in black.

The youngest ones in the house can help by crumpling up the paper... We're sure they'll have a great time!

23

DRAWINGS
on a smooth surface

The ideal bases for this project are non-porous surfaces. We give you some ideas in the materials section.

MATERIALS: A smooth surface (a floor tile, window, plastic chopping board, or plastic sleeve...), paints, a roller, a plastic paint tray, cotton swabs, paper (white and colored), and a pencil.

1 Make a few drawings on a sheet of paper. Practice the one you like the most, because you'll have to draw it directly. They must be very simple outline shapes.

1

2

2 Now pour some paint into the paint tray. Wet the roller and paint a square on the smooth surface you picked.

24

3 Quickly, before the paint dries, make the outline you thought of with a cotton swab.

4 Put a sheet of paper over the drawing and remove it quickly. You'll see that you end up with a reverse image of your original drawing, so keep this in mind if you draw letters.

You've just made a monotype. That's what this printing technique is called.

25

You can make any kind of drawing you can think of. Here, we suggest a t-shirt with faces, which will look great on you, for sure!

FACES on clothing

MATERIALS: A t-shirt (or another piece of fabric), fabric paints, paintbrushes, a tray or paint for mixing colors, a black fabric marker, newspapers or cardboard the same size as the t-shirt, pencil or water-based pen, and bottle caps.

1 Draw some funny faces on a sheet of paper and, when you decide which ones you like the best, draw the circles you want by tracing around a cap with a pencil. Draw the faces inside.

2 Now you get your t-shirt ready for painting. Put newspaper or cardboard inside it so you don't get the back dirty when you paint.

1

2

3 Prepare the fabric paints, putting a little of the colors you want into a dish. Paint carefully to avoid going outside the lines. Use the tip of the paintbrush to define the outsides of the circles.

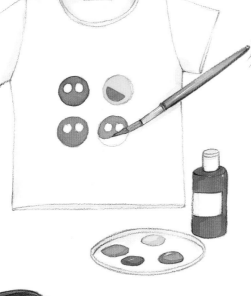

4 Finish by outlining the faces with a black fabric pen. If you go over the line a little, it will be hidden. Now you can take the cardboard out and try it on. Do you like it?

Fabric paints are special. You can wash them and they don't come off, but before washing, you need to iron them to set the color.

A CATERPILLAR
on tracing paper

With tracing paper, you can copy any drawings you like and then give them a personal touch.

MATERIALS: Tracing paper, felt tip pens, sheets of paper, pencil, paper clips, and different-sized bottle caps.

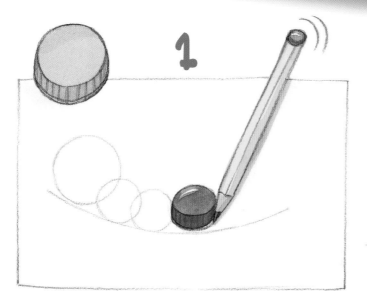

1 Make a pencil drawing on a sheet of paper. For this nice caterpillar, we have drawn overlapping circles using different-sized caps.

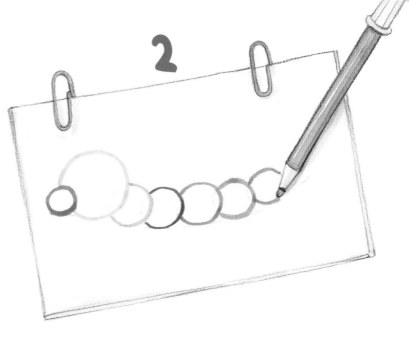

2 Place the tracing paper over your drawing and secure it with paper clips. Copy the drawing onto the tracing paper with the felt-tip pens. Start with the outline, but remember not to draw the entire circle, so that they overlap (see the illustration).

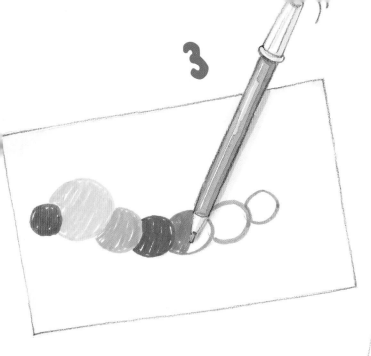

3 Color the inside of the circles the same colors as the outlines. To obtain a uniform color with the pen, hold the pen sideways and move from top to bottom with parallel lines, very close together but without going outside the lines.

4 After you finish coloring the caterpillar, add the details you like: eyes, mouth, antennae, legs, the ground and plants… Be creative!

Markers slide really easily over the tracing paper and you can also copy whatever drawing you like.

FOOD on foam

MATERIALS: Foam (EVA), scissors, pencil, a plate, acrylic paints, and a paintbrush.

What about some appetizing mouse pads for your computer? Or mats to decorate the kitchen wall?

2

1

1 Think about which food you want to make and find some foam in the color that's best for your food. If you're going to cut out a slice of watermelon, you can trace around a plate to draw a half-circle.

2 Cut the foam along the line you made.

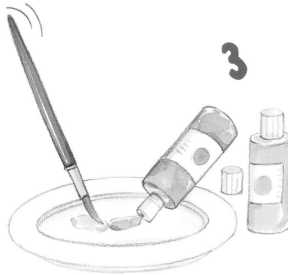

3 Prepare the paint you need to decorate it. You can mix the colors in a small dish.

4 Now you can paint the details on with a paintbrush so that your food looks real: The seeds in the watermelon, the holes in the cheese…

If you're going to use them as mouse pads, don't decorate them too much, so that your mouse moves over it easily. Just add a few key details.

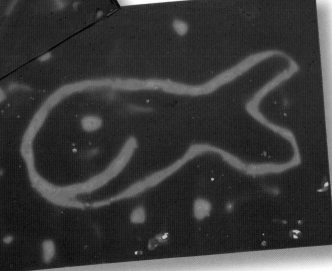

A BLACKBOARD
on a paint-filled sleeve

MATERIALS: A plastic sleeve (for paper), scissors, paints, and sticky tape.

Your friends will love this blackboard… and it's so easy!

1 Find a soft plastic sleeve for paper and cut a rectangle out of it. Close three sides with strips of folded transparent tape (slightly longer than the sleeve, so you can fold over the ends). So in the end you should have a bag open on one side.

2 Squeeze a little paint into the open side, without overdoing it! Spread it out with your hand and add a little more if necessary, making sure that the paint doesn't leak out.

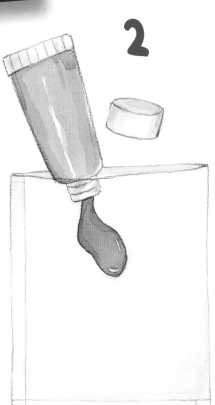

3 Spread the paint out with your hand until the whole inside of the bag is covered with a very fine layer of color. There shouldn't be any gaps or air bubbles. Close the bag tightly with a piece of tape and go over the edges and corners well so that the paint cannot leak out anywhere.

4 Spread the paint out again with your hand and your blackboard is ready! Draw what you like with your finger. You know how to erase the drawing, don't you? Of course! By smoothing out the paint again with your hand!

No pencils, or pens, or scissors... A finger is all you need to draw.

There are always windows nearby to decorate. You can illustrate the arrival of spring, or the start of vacations!

FLOWERS
on glass

1 Practice drawing on a windowpane. You can erase and change the drawing until you decide what drawing you want to make.

MATERIALS: A pane of glass (from a picture or a window), a white or colored glass pen (that can be erased), paper, pencil, and a sheet of colored card.

2 When you've decided, make a pencil drawing on a sheet of paper.

3 Put it under the glass and trace it with the glass pen.

4 To finish the painting, you could put a colored card behind it so that your drawing stands out more. If you get tired of the color, change it. And if you get tired of the drawing, simply erase it and make a new one!

Using this technique, you can redecorate whenever you want. Just erase the drawing, make another one and it's ready.

First edition for North America published in 2015 by
Barron's Educational Series, Inc.
Original title of the book in Catalan: *L'art de pintar sobre diferents supports*
© Copyright GEMSER PUBLICATIONS S.L., 2015
c/Castell, 38; Teià(0829) Barcelona, Spain (World Rights)
Tel: 93 540 13 53
E-mail: *info@mercedesros.com*
Website: *www.mercedesros.com*
Author and illustrator: Bernadette Cuxart

ISBN: 978-1-4380-0651-2
Library of Congress Control No.: 2014949910

All inquiries should be addressed to:
Barron's Educational Series, Inc.
250 Wireless Boulevard
Hauppauge, NY 11788
www.barronseduc.com

Printed in China
9 8 7 6 5 4 3 2 1

Date of Manufacture: January 2015
Place of Manufacture: L. REX PRINTING COMPANY
    LIMITED, Dongguan City, Guangdong, China